Suzuki
Flute School
Volume 4 Piano Part
by Toshio Takahashi

© 1999, 1971 Dr. Shinichi Suzuki
Sole publisher for the entire world except Japan:
Summy-Birchard Inc.
exclusively distributed by
Warner Bros. Publications
15800 N.W. 48th Avenue, Miami, Florida 33014
All rights reserved   Printed in U.S.A.

ISBN 0-87487-172-7

INTRODUCTION

FOR THE STUDENT: This material is part of the worldwide Suzuki Method of teaching. Companion recordings should be used with these publications. In addition, there are flute part books that go along with this material.

FOR THE TEACHER: In order to be an effective Suzuki teacher, a great deal of ongoing education is required. Your national Suzuki association provides this for its membership. Teachers are encouraged to become members of their national Suzuki associations and maintain a teacher training schedule, in order to remain current, via institutes, short-term programs and long-term programs. You are also encouraged to join the International Suzuki Association.

FOR THE PARENT: Credentials are essential for any teacher you choose. We recommend you ask your teacher for his or her credentials, especially those relating to training in the Suzuki Method. The Suzuki Method experience should be a positive one, where there exists a wonderful, fostering relationship between child, parent and teacher. So choosing the right teacher is of the utmost importance.

In order to obtain more information about the Suzuki Method, please contact your country's Suzuki Association; the International Suzuki Association at 3-10-15 Fukashi, Matsumoto City 390, Japan; The Suzuki Association of the Americas, P.O. Box 17310, Boulder, Colorado 80308; or Summy-Birchard Inc., c/o Warner Bros. Publications, 15800 N.W. 48th Avenue, Miami, Florida 33014, for current Associations' addresses.

CONTENTS

1   **Menuet,** *J. S. Bach* 5

2   **Siciliano,** *J. S. Bach* 8

3   **Minuet from Sonata III,** *G. F. Handel* 11

4   **Allegro from Sonata III,** *G. F. Handel* 12

5   **Sonata II,** *M. Blavet*

      Andante 16

      Allemande 19

      Gavotte 21

      Sarabande 23

      Finale 24

1
Menuetto メヌエット

from "Sonata IV" 「ソナタ第4番」から

J. S. Bach
バッハ

6

Menuetto I Da Capo

2
Siciliano シチリアーノ
from "Sonata II" 「ソナタ第2番」から

J. S. Bach
バッハ

3

Minuet
from "Sonata III"

メヌエット

「ソナタ第3番」から

G.F. Handel
ヘンデル

4

Allegro
from "Sonata III"

アレグロ

「ソナタ第3番」から

G.F. Handel
ヘンデル

5

Sonata II

ソナタ第2番

M. Blavet
ブラベー

Allemande

Allegro (♩ = 120)

Gavotte (les caquets)

Tranquillo (♩=90)

Finale
Allegro ($\quarternote = 126$)